IMAGES
of America

TRUSSVILLE

The Cahaba River begins north of Trussville, flowing through several communities before joining the Alabama River to the south. A major water source over the centuries for Native Americans and wildlife, it provided an ideal settlement spot for homesteaders during the early 1800s. One of the nation's most unique rivers, it is the longest free-flowing river in Alabama and is home to a variety of aquatic and plant life. (Courtesy of John Shadrick.)

ON THE COVER: The Trussville Fire Department, begun in 1947 as an all-volunteer unit, started out with a 1942 Dodge fire engine purchased for $9,000 by the Trussville Civitan Club. These men are but a few of the many individuals who have expended time and effort over the years to serve and protect the citizens of Trussville. Today's Trussville Fire & Rescue is comprised of 40 full-time employees and 70 volunteers. The old Dodge is still in the department's fleet. (Courtesy of Earl and Carol Massey.)

IMAGES
of America

TRUSSVILLE

Sandra Bearden and June Mathews

ARCADIA
PUBLISHING

Published by Arcadia Publishing
Charleston, South Carolina

Library of Congress Control Number: 2013944830

For all general information, please contact Arcadia Publishing:
Telephone 843-853-2070
Fax 843-853-0044
E-mail sales@arcadiapublishing.com
For customer service and orders:
Toll-Free 1-888-313-2665

Visit us on the Internet at www.arcadiapublishing.com

*This book is gratefully dedicated to our civic forebears,
whose character, service, perseverance, and faith created the
cornerstone for the Trussville we live in and love today.*

CONTENTS

ACKNOWLEDGMENTS

This book is a snapshot of life in Trussville from roughly the mid-1930s, when families began moving into the new homes of the Cahaba Project, until the mid-1960s, when the seeds of progress were showing signs of taking root and growing.

From the experience of compiling this collection of vintage photographs, we have learned that (to paraphrase an oft-quoted saying) it indeed takes a village to create a pictorial history. Thus, we are indebted to several of our fellow villagers, past and present, for their parts in making it happen.

Many of the photographs on the following pages were provided by Earl and Carol Massey, long considered the premier historians of Trussville and surrounding areas. As chronologers of local lore, we pale in comparison, so we are honored by their willingness to contribute to our effort. Unless otherwise indicated, the images in this book came to us through them.

As you browse through the book, you'll see the names of other families, individuals, and entities that donated time, photographs, and information to the cause. Their contributions are also much appreciated.

Gratitude is due to Emily Tish and her staff at the Trussville Public Library for opening their archives room to us and for letting us ramble through the material there. We also appreciate Don Veasey for unearthing scads of Trussville-related photographs and documents from within the Birmingham Public Library Archives. And, we thank Tim Pennycuff, university archivist at the University of Alabama at Birmingham, for the use of images from UAB's collection.

Not in a million years could we have produced this number of photographic files in the proper publisher-required format without the assistance of Stephanie Entrup. Her ability to efficiently scan and format saved us much time and many a headache, and for that we are tremendously grateful.

Many thanks to the Arcadia team for their patience and guidance throughout the process. They made our first foray into the book-publishing world a relatively painless experience and what we hope will become a roaring success.

And, last but far from least, a heartfelt "Thank You" to Bill Bearden and Jimmie Mathews for their unwavering support and encouragement. We could not have done it without them.

INTRODUCTION

The Cahaba River was there before man. For centuries, it has flowed through Alabama, brushing the edge of the Appalachian highlands, then slashing through forest canopies and sunny glades as it flows southward to join the Alabama River and then the Gulf of Mexico.

Near its headwaters, in north central Alabama, the Cahaba is continually changing. At places, it is a raging river, felling trees and swallowing everything in its path. At other spots, it is a tiny trickle that barely shines in the summer sun. Again, it is an ordinary forest stream, offering refreshment and relief to thirsty animals and humans.

Over the centuries, wildlife has come to drink from the Cahaba River and to prey on fellow creatures. In earlier times, Native Americans hunted, fished, and camped along its banks. Evidence of their presence has been found in the form of broken pottery, arrows, and other artifacts.

More centuries passed, but the river changed little. Then, after the American Revolution, thousands of settlers poured in from the Carolinas, Virginia, Georgia, and other parts of the newly formed United States. They were seeking land of their own for growing cotton, corn, and other crops. By 1817, land surrounding the river was part of a new US territory. In 1819, the territory, named Alabama, became the 22nd state to enter the Union.

Among those immigrating to Alabama from other states and abroad was Warren Truss, a North Carolinian who settled in the area when it was still a territory. Truss eventually owned nearly 1,000 acres of land in what is now Jefferson County, Alabama. He built a gristmill by the river to accommodate settlers who were clearing the forests to plant cotton, corn, oats, vegetables, and other crops.

A small community that came to be known as Truss grew up around the gristmill and the river. Although the divisive issue of slavery was beginning to split the nation, there were no large plantations around Truss. While a few landowners near the village had slaves, small farmers and their families mainly tilled the land themselves. However, when the Civil War started, many men and boys joined local regiments out of loyalty to their state and to protect their land.

Relatively unscathed, postwar Trussville prospered. Its residents were hard-working people with useful skills, and the literacy rate in town was far above that for the county. Some of that could be credited to Prof. R.G. Hewitt, whose leadership in education made a lasting impression throughout the area. Today, two Trussville schools still bear his name.

In addition to its school, local churches helped the little hamlet become a true cohesive community. Many of those early churches have grown and flourished, attracting crowds of worshippers as the tiny town blossomed into a city.

Another strong influence was nearby Birmingham, a city born after the Civil War. Birmingham would one day produce 40 percent of the nation's pig iron. The railroads had come; the iron and coal industries were booming locally; and Trussville joined in. A blast furnace went up along the edge of the Cahaba River in the late 1880s, and the river's clear water was soon sullied with the debris of pig-iron production. But, the town's ventures into heavy industry died, and the Trussville furnace closed after World War I.

The 20th century, the age of the automobile, and the development of Birmingham helped Trussville's evolution from isolation to urbanization. Although this trend began in the 1920s, it took a giant step through, of all things, the Great Depression. During Franklin D. Roosevelt's administration, the federal government developed a government-funded, planned suburban community.

Originally called Slag Heap Village, after the slag pile left by the blast furnace, the development soon received a new name: Cahaba Village. Ultimately, locals would call it Cahaba Project, or "the Project." Completed just prior to World War II, the Project functioned as a separate community from "old Trussville" until June 1947, when the town of Trussville was officially born.

It would be another quarter century before other major changes occurred in Trussville. The completion of Interstates 1-59 and I-459 in the 1970s and 1980s eased commutes and attracted home buyers. Though Trussville was still distinctive, it was not quite as remote. By the 1980s, Trussville was bringing additional land into the city limits and working with business developers to provide a broader tax base for expanded city services.

At the turn of the 21st century, Trussville continued its transformation from an isolated rural hamlet to a distinctive small city that has become the hub of northeastern metropolitan Birmingham. Afternoon traffic crowds once-deserted Main Street, and modern shopping centers have replaced the old general store, but Trussville has retained the small-town ambience and family-friendly atmosphere that attract new residents and retain old ones.

While this pictorial history touches on the distant past and the present, it focuses on the middle of the 20th century, which set the pattern for what Trussville is today.

One

THE EARLY DAYS

Warren Truss (shown here) and his brother Joel, along with their families, settled in central Alabama sometime before 1820. Around 1821, Warren bought land in Jefferson County on the banks of the Cahaba River, where he built a gristmill. He also erected a log building for use as a school, meetinghouse, and church. The growing settlement was named for him.

A2-1389-1

Although there is some dispute regarding its exact age, there is no doubt the historic Hickman-Yarbrough-Parrish house is one of Trussville's oldest and best-preserved treasures. Native Americans once camped on nearby land bought by W.P. Hickman in the 1850s, about the time he married Elvira Hamilton. The house, built with slave labor, was once the center of a vast Hickman estate. Legend has it that the Hickman house was the only one left standing in the area when Wilson's Raiders came through in April 1865, because Hickman was a Mason and so were some of the Yankee officers. His son Cunningham Wilson Hickman lived in the house until 1944, when he sold it to the W.P. Yarbroughs. This photograph shows the original mansard roof, which was altered sometime in the early 20th century. (Courtesy of Dave and Joni Parrish.)

W.P. Hickman sits on the porch of the home he built in Trussville. After the Civil War, he served as assistant treasurer of Jefferson County for many years. Sold by his son to the W.P. Yarbroughs in the 1940s, the house stayed in that family another half century, as Mrs. Yarbrough lived to be 100. It was nearly the 21st century when the Parrish family bought it. (Courtesy of Dave and Joni Parrish.)

John Spearman Edwards, the earliest known physician to practice in Trussville, built this two-story frame house after the Civil War, possibly around 1879. With chimneys at each end, foursquare columns, and a pitched tin roof, the home replaced a cruder log cabin on the property. According to *Historic Sites of Jefferson County*, Edwards bought his land in the area from Warren Truss. The book states that the log smokehouse, visible in the background, was built before the Civil War with slave labor, although the house itself was constructed after the war. George Edwards, the last family member to own the property, sold the house in 1946. Later, it was moved to Tannehill State Park as an example of mid-19th-century dwellings in Alabama.

The Trussville City Cemetery, originally the Cahawba Baptist Cemetery, was the site of the church, which was organized in 1821 and later moved. Many of the names in the cemetery are those of early settlers, including Mr. and Mrs. James Glenn (above) and Dr. Samuel Acton (below). Other names familiar to the area, including Melton, Sims, McCrory, and Truss, are on headstones in the cemetery. Among those buried here is Warren Truss, for whom the city is named. Although the city maintains the grounds, time has weathered and degraded some of the markers. The cemetery is at 130 Main Street, across from city hall. (Both courtesy of Sandra Bearden.)

A number of headstones in Trussville City Cemetery are marked with Confederate flags, signifying the final resting places of Southern veterans. Among these are Capt. Thomas King Truss (above) and Capt. Joseph Martin (below). They were among the hundreds of eastern Jefferson County men who responded to the call to arms after the Battle of Fort Sumter. The central Alabama men would fight the long war in faraway battles, however. The devastation of war did not affect Jefferson County as much as it did much of the Deep South. (Both courtesy of Sandra Bearden.)

Although many Trussville men left home to fight, and in some cases die, for the Confederacy, Trussville itself was untouched by the Union army until April 20, 1865—after Lee's surrender to Grant at Appomattox Courthouse, Virginia. This marker describes the day that a Union detachment swooped down and burned the Confederate storehouse at Trussville. The marker stands at the corner of Highway 11 and North Chalkville Road.

CONFEDERATE STOREHOUSE BURNED BY FEDERAL TROOPS
April 20, 1865

On this site stood the stone warehouse of Captain Thomas Truss and Marcus Worthington. Stored here were meats, grains and clothing collected by the Confederate government as a war tax. Disabled C. S. A. veteran Felix M. Wood was receiver of the tax at Trussville. The building was burned by a detachment of Wilson's Raiders under the command of John T. Croxton. Brigadier General U. S. Volunteers.

ERECTED 1955 BY THE TRUSSVILLE HISTORICAL BOARD

This is a later version of the mill Warren Truss built when he settled in central Alabama. Munger Mill was located on the headwaters of the Cahaba River, about five miles north of Trussville. Constructed in the 1870s, the complex included a sawmill, gristmill, and cotton gin. Wooden piles at the water's edge and sandstone slabs in the back supported the building, and a wooden water wheel was linked to the grist operation inside the house. In 1925, Mrs. R.S. Munger donated the mill and 65 acres of surrounding land to the YWCA. It was a girls' camp for about the next 40 years. (Courtesy of Birmingham, Alabama Public Library Archives.)

John Daniel Sinkler Davis, born in Trussville, was only two years old when his father, Dr. Elias Davis, left to serve and die for the Confederacy in the Civil War. The younger Davis, however, chose to follow the family profession, graduating from the Medical College of Georgia. He served as president of the Jefferson County Medical Association and was active in other professional medical organizations. He is an inductee in the Alabama Healthcare Hall of Fame. (Courtesy of UAB Lister Hill Library, University of Alabama at Birmingham.)

Dr. William Elias Brownlee Davis, brother of J.D.S. Davis, was born while his father served in the Confederate army. He began his medical studies at Vanderbilt University and completed them at Bellevue Medical College in New York City. He was a founder of the *Alabama Medical and Surgical Journal* and was regarded as one of the state's outstanding surgeons. He is a member of the Alabama Healthcare Hall of Fame. (Courtesy of UAB Lister Hill Library, University of Alabama at Birmingham.)

With the industrialization of the new city of Birmingham came the railroads. And, the railroads came to Trussville. From the 1890s until the middle of the 20th century, railways built housing for workers along sections of railroad tracks. In some cases, such buildings were used for storing equipment. This section house in the Trussville area was built by the Alabama Great Southern Railroad.

The Trussville blast furnace was one of 27 built in Alabama during the 1880s, signaling the beginning of modern pig-iron manufacturing in the state, especially in and around Birmingham. The village of Trussville joined this trend in 1887, when the Birmingham Furnace & Manufacturing Co. rebuilt a dismantled furnace from Pennsylvania on the banks of the Cahaba River. Manufacturing began, and owners built homes for workers.

The Trussville Furnace operated intermittently over a period of three decades, from 1889 until 1919, under a half-dozen ownerships. This is the Lacey-Buck Iron Company commissary about 1902. The Lacey-Buck operation continued until it was bought by Southern Steel in 1906. But, any Trussville dreams of becoming a steel town soon died. The high cost of raw-material transportation hampered the operation.

By the late 1920s, when this photograph was probably taken, the Trussville Furnace had been dormant for a decade. Couples, such as Nellie Pullen Vann and her friend, a Mr. Massey, used the furnace buildings as a photographic backdrop. The structure was dismantled in 1933, when the land was sold to the federal government. (Courtesy of Ruth Robison.)

This Trussville rock quarry, shown in operation with wagons and animals in the early 1900s, was owned by John Warren Worthington & Company. Worthington, along with his brother Thomas and H.F. Debardeleben, quarried limestone, mined ore, and developed railroads. Debardeleben has been acknowledged as a leader in helping Birmingham become the industrial capital of the New South in the early 20th century.

When settlers moved into Alabama to farm, they generally viewed forests as obstacles. By the end of the 19th century, however, there was a boom in the timber industry. In Trussville, as shown here, loggers and lumbermen transported logs from the woods to the sawmills using animal-drawn carts and wagons. By the early 20th century, logging crews had changed from part-time farmers to full-time workers.

Sawmills were among the first industries established in newly settled areas, and they quickly became established as important to their communities. During much of the 19th and early 20th centuries, many Alabama sawmills were family-owned operations, like Roper's Sawmill, located south of the railroad tracks and across from the train station in Trussville. This photograph illustrates that mules were still a dominant power source in the sawmill industry.

By the dawn of the 20th century, a growing number of middle-class Trussville residents—merchants, professional people, and prosperous farmers—enjoyed a comfortable but unpretentious lifestyle and had some leisure time. Among the homes in the community were those of S.R. McDanal (above), editor of the *Trussville Life* newspaper in the 1890s, and the Hendon house (below) on Clay Road, a turn-of-the-century version of today's garden home. But, this one probably had a garden!

It is every child's dream to ride a pony, preferably one with a flowing headdress (most likely a decorative fly sheet). Shown here is W.L. Martin's stable on Hickman Road (now North Chalkville Road). The occasion may be a birthday party. If so, it was a family event, for everyone in the photograph is named Martin, with the exception of Tobe, the man at center holding the reins of a horse.

Is this a 50th-anniversary celebration for the couple standing in front of the tree? Is it a birthday party for the boy in the sailor suit or maybe a family reunion? Whatever the occasion, this festive get-together of an unidentified group was photographed in rural Trussville early in the 20th century.

This group may resemble Huck Finn, Aunt Polly, and friends; more likely, it is a group of Trussville ladies and a boy interested in having fresh fish for supper. The Cahaba River has long been a source of water and wildlife for residents. This photograph, taken in the early 20th century, shows the ongoing popularity of fishing on a lazy summer afternoon in Alabama.

Two

THE CAHABA PROJECT

This stone bridge was built during the construction of the Cahaba Project, a New Deal planned community that transformed Trussville. Spanning the Cahaba River, the bridge's purpose was to connect sections of the Cahaba Project. Planners decided not to build north of the river, however, leaving only undeveloped land as the destination. Some locals called the bridge "Roosevelt's Folly." Years later, homes, a school, and parks were developed north of the Cahaba. (Courtesy of Ron Burkett.)

The country town of Trussville is seen here around 1930. The houses were built for blast furnace employees before the facility was abandoned. The Great Depression, hard on almost everyone, was especially difficult for those who had little to begin with. Pres. Franklin Roosevelt's New Deal programs were designed to aid the South and other economically depressed areas. One agency, the Resettlement Administration, had the goal of improving living conditions in poor farming areas. In the Birmingham area, local citizens such as Robert Jemison Jr. and Charles Debardeleben were involved in selecting five sites for such construction, as was Rexford G. Tugwell, the US assistant secretary of agriculture, a top Roosevelt advisor. After an inspection tour, Tugwell dubbed the Trussville location Slag Heap Village because of the slag piles remaining from the 750-acre blast furnace site. Tugwell considered the Trussville site unsuitable for farming, but appropriate for residential development. Fortunately, the name was soon altered to Cahaba Village and ultimately to the Cahaba Project.

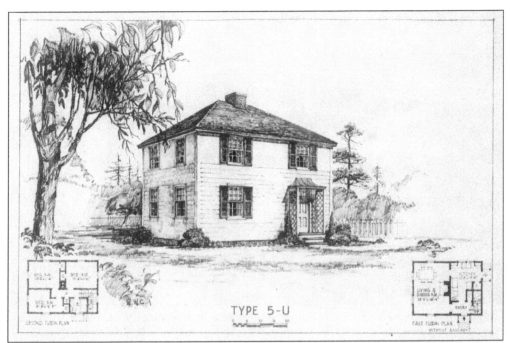

TYPE 5-U

The men largely responsible for planning the Cahaba Project were W.H. Kessler, a landscape architect who was considered the town planner, and D.H. Greer, the architect. Greer designed several house plans before narrowing the selection, dispersing selected designs throughout the development. This rendering shows plans for a two-story, single-family dwelling. Variations on two-story duplexes and one-story, single-family homes also were in the plans.

The Cahaba Project and other government housing programs not only provided homes, but also badly needed jobs. Once Resettlement Administration authorities approved the plans in 1936, construction got under way. A call went out for skilled, semi-skilled, and unskilled workers, ranging from 40¢-per-hour laborers to $2-per-hour tractor owner-operators, like the one shown clearing land. The total allotted budget was $2.7 million.

Things began to take shape once buildings and workers' houses from the old blast furnace site were razed, and all evidence of the industrial past began to be replaced by a suburban community. Scenes such as this one were familiar, as workers, ranging from cement finishers to road builders, labored feverishly. The Cahaba Project was the last and largest of the Birmingham-area government housing projects.

This is one of the larger homes in the Cahaba Project. Homes had indoor plumbing, electricity, hot and cold running water, separate garages, and other modern amenities. Each home was situated on a spacious lot, providing home garden and recreational space. The government set parameters on income for occupants, with monthly rental rates ranging from $14 to $23, according to family size. Applications began to pour in.

Meanwhile, the old blast furnace was demolished, and land was cleared for a new high school and adjacent co-operative building, both to be built at the edge of the Cahaba River. Placed in the heart of the Project overlooking a spacious mall area flanked by two-story houses, the school and co-op would be the centers of activity for the community. Hewitt High School opened in 1938.

The first families moved into Project homes in 1938, and by January 1941 the population was about 1,000 people. A strong community soon developed, with the co-op building as the hub. The co-operative store featured amenities needed by all residents, including a grocery, beauty shop, barbershop, filling station, and washing machines. Some ladies even formed a unique sorority emerging from friendships formed using the machines; they called it "Sisters of the Suds."

In many ways, the Cahaba Project was ahead of its time. This structure, the Gazebo, was built to designate the entrance to the Project, just as many modern subdivisions have special entrances and gateways. Purely unintentional, the Gazebo also symbolized some barriers that existed between old Trussville and Project residents. Many residents of the older community, especially those lacking indoor plumbing and using well-drawn water, may have been a bit envious of the development some called the "government's country club." But, schools and a newspaper edited by Wilmer Lamons, the *Trussville Times*, helped the two communities bond. By 1947, the government put Project homes up for sale, and many tenants bought the houses they occupied. Returning veterans also were eager to buy. The two communities—the Project residents and the people of old Trussville—merged to incorporate as the town of Trussville in July 1947. (Courtesy of John Shadrick.)

Three

FAMILY LIFE

Teddy Gilmer and Imelda Walrond met at Hewitt High School. They continued dating and were married on February 18, 1956, during Gilmer's senior year at Georgia Tech. They are shown here following the ceremony at Taylor Memorial Methodist Church. After Gilmer graduated and served two years in the Army in Aberdeen, Maryland, the couple bought a Project home in Trussville. (Courtesy of Imelda Gilmer.)

The Gilmers' first home had two bedrooms and one bath—tiny by today's standards. It was plenty big for newlyweds, though, and convenient to their widening circle of friends, their church, and community events. Danna, their first child, had plenty of space, but with the arrival of daughter Joy and son Ted, the family moved to larger quarters. They did not dream of leaving Trussville. (Courtesy of Imelda Gilmer.)

Enjoying a rare Alabama snow in the early 1960s are the Gilmer daughters Joy (left) and Danna, with their father, Teddy. Postwar Project kids were baby boomers with plenty of other children around and areas for playing outdoors all seasons of the year, from swim meets to snowball fights. (Courtesy of Imelda Gilmer.)

Lully Wheeler (standing) reigned over the "Lullybye Kindergarten" during the 1960s. A benevolent but absolute ruler in her classroom, she helped mold the minds and manners of several generations of Trussville preschoolers. Danna Gilmer (first row, third from left) was among them. Many Lullybye graduates went through school together and have remained fast friends all their lives. (Courtesy of Imelda Gilmer.)

Imelda Gilmer, holding baby Ted, dressed her girls Joy (left) and Danna in identical outfits for their first flight, a trip to Memphis; even the baby is wearing his Sunday best. Although people may have worn less casual travel outfits in the 1960s, there was much less red tape associated with getting on planes. (Courtesy of Imelda Gilmer.)

One familiar name around old Trussville was Bradford. The Paul Bradford family lived next door to the elementary school, a convenient location for the family's three children and close to Mr. and Mrs. Bradford's work. Shown here enjoying a snowy day are Gloria Bradford (left) and Cissy Edwards, with their dog Lady. (Courtesy of Gloria Bradford Forehand.)

Paul E. Bradford and Lisala Todd Bradford spent more time together than most married couples. During their long marriage, they also worked together for 37 years. He was the postmaster and she the postal clerk in the post office, on the lower level of this building, which was owned by the Masonic lodge. Paul later served as grand master of Masons for the state of Alabama and was a founder of Cahaba Bank & Trust. (Courtesy of Gloria Bradford Forehand.)

Showing enthusiasm for their job are Paul E. Bradford Sr. (left), Rev. Richard Francis (center), and Gerald Bradford. The men are breaking ground for a new sanctuary at First Baptist Church, Trussville. Gerald Bradford worked as an engineer for Alabama Power Company. He and his father were on the building committee for the church project, which was completed in 1967. (Courtesy of Gloria Bradford Forehand.)

Old Trussville and Project kids had a common love for the swimming area on the Cahaba River formed by this dam. Gloria Forehand remembers using a rope hanging from a tree to swing out over the water. Parents usually allowed teens to swim at the dam if they could prove they were good enough swimmers and, as one adolescent of that time said, "if we'd had our typhoid shots." (Courtesy of Gloria Bradford Forehand.)

Barbie and R.W. "Mac" McLendon met during World War II, when Mac was stationed in Ohio as a Navy pilot. His job was to ferry planes from manufacturing plants to air bases on the West and East Coasts. He always returned to Columbus, where he fell in love with the beautiful Barbara Finley. When they married in 1942, Barbie had just graduated from Denison University. Soon after their marriage, Mac was stricken with polio and was treated at Warm Springs, Georgia. He later completely recovered. Mac had grown up in Birmingham's West End, so in 1947 the McLendons decided to move south. Driving into the Birmingham area, they passed through Trussville. The Cahaba Project had what the couple was looking for: affordable housing in a quiet community. Mac attended Birmingham-Southern College on the GI Bill to complete the education he had begun at the University of Alabama before the war. While at BSC, Mac also worked as a real estate appraiser. (Courtesy of Laurie McLendon Nabors.)

The McLendons' first home was on Rockridge Avenue in the Project, and that is where they brought home their first child, Laurie, in 1949; Tommy, Cissy, and Tuck came later. The McLendons immediately became involved in the community, from social clubs to church activities. Such involvement had been a way of life in the Project since it was completed, and both established residents and newcomers were proud that their community was regarded as a model city. (Courtesy of Laurie McLendon Nabors.)

Playing in the sandbox on a typical summer day in the early 1950s are, from left to right, cousin Barbara Sykes and Laurie, Cissy, and Tommy McLendon. All were members of the baby boomer generation, and the baby business was booming in the Project. The McLendons had moved into a two-story house on South Mall, and dozens of children lived in the neighborhood. (Courtesy of Laurie McLendon Nabors.)

In the 1950s and 1960s, little girls (and their mothers) dressed up for parties, as evidenced by this group of young ladies attending an outdoor birthday celebration. With an average of one car per family and bus service between Trussville and downtown Birmingham running only twice daily, the ladies and children kept close to home. But, within the confines of Trussville, which had a population of 2,700 in 1960, children had freedom to play in the spacious yards and parks of the town. (Courtesy of Laurie McLendon Nabors.)

Mac McLendon kept busy with his job at First Federal Savings & Loan Association in Birmingham and his elected post in Trussville as an alderman. Trussville had incorporated as a town in 1947, blending the Project and old Trussville into one unit. Posing in this early-1950s photograph are, from left to right, (first row) McLendon, Ald. John C. Yarbrough, and Ald. Richard Beard; (second row) Ald. Henry T. Rodgers, Mayor Horace Norrell, and Ald. George Glenn Sr. (Courtesy of Laurie McLendon Nabors.)

Not all Project families were homegrown. Henry Woodfin Grady Lancaster was a North Carolinian, and Frances Annamay Nickell Lancaster was from Missouri. They met at Oklahoma A&M (now Oklahoma State University), marrying in 1921. After graduation, Henry taught school before going to work for the US Department of Agriculture in Chicago. The USDA transferred him to Birmingham in 1938. When he heard of the new Cahaba Project, he investigated, liked what he saw, and bid on a two-story rental house. The bid was accepted, and the family moved into the Project in June 1938. (Courtesy of Carol Lancaster Massey.)

By 1946, there were eight children in the Lancaster family, three of them born as native Trussvillians. Shown here are, from left to right, (first row) Virginia (holding Robert), Carol, Juanita Jo, Grady, and Marilyn; (second row) Ken and Dorothy. Idle moments were unknown to the Lancaster children, as their parents saw that they studied hard in school, and they all took piano lessons. There was plenty of work to round out their days. The girls learned early to assist their mother with cooking, cleaning, and caring for younger brothers and sisters. The boys helped their dad with outside chores. (Courtesy of Carol Lancaster Massey.)

With a large family to feed, Grady Lancaster asked permission from the federal government to garden and raise domestic animals on about 40 acres of land adjacent to the Project home they were renting; permission was granted. The government had bought the land, shown in these photographs with Lancaster on horseback, but had not included it in the Project. When they were not in school, kids helped tend a garden and look after animals, including cattle, horses, turkeys, pigs, chickens, and rabbits. When the property became available for sale, the Lancasters bought it. Years later, after the death of both parents, the heirs developed the property into the Lancashire subdivision. (Both courtesy of Carol Lancaster Massey.)

Although some of the Lancaster siblings never moved from the Trussville area, others left but ultimately came back. One was Grady, the oldest Lancaster son, who lived outside the United States frequently and did not return to Trussville as a permanent resident for 22 years. He had graduated from Hewitt High School at age 16 and enlisted in the US Army at 17, ultimately serving hitches in Korea, Japan, stateside, and Germany and fighting in the Korean War. While stationed in Japan, he met Shizuko Fujii. This photograph shows Grady and Shizuko on their wedding day, December 26, 1951. The couple had four children, three of them born abroad. After Grady left the service, the family moved to Trussville and built a house on Lancaster land, and Grady went to work for the Social Security Administration. He served on the Trussville City Council from 1980 to 1988. Shizuko died in 1994, and Grady married a former classmate, Betty Ann Milner Swift, who died in 2012. (Courtesy of Grady Lancaster.)

Chatting at the Junior L'Amica Club's 1949 dance are, from left to right, Leroy "Gus" Kennedy, Mary Louise Swatzell (incoming club president), Jeannine Roberts (outgoing president), and Richard Beard. Kennedy and Swatzell met at a "backward" party when she was 16 and he was 21. By that time, Kennedy had served a hitch in the Navy. By the time Swatzell was 16, she and Kennedy were engaged. They married three years later. (Courtesy of Mary Louise Swatzell Kennedy.)

Gus and Mary Kennedy made their home in Trussville and had two daughters, Donna and Cheri. Like their parents, the girls enjoyed the freedom of living in a small, close-knit community. Many children's activities revolved around school and church. Here, girls are dressed in settlers' garb to commemorate the 1821 founding of First Baptist Church, Trussville. (Courtesy of Mary Louise Swatzell Kennedy.)

The Kennedys moved into a Project house on Rockridge Avenue soon after their marriage. In 1969, they bought a larger home just outside the Project. There, they were still close enough to participate in church and other community activities. Years later, Gus was on the board at Trussville's Senior Center, where the couple made close friends. One highlight was playing Mr. and Mrs. Santa Claus in the city Christmas parade, an annual event sponsored by the city and the Trussville Area Chamber of Commerce. Mary Louise remembers sitting under the newly lighted city Christmas tree, helping Santa take requests. "One little girl plopped into my lap and said she wanted a baby sister for Christmas," said the Mrs. Claus stand-in. "I was trying to frame a response when her mother came up, pregnant and obviously close to delivery. I breathed a sigh of relief." (Courtesy of Mary Louise Swatzell Kennedy.)

The white house in the photograph above was the first building used by Tom Crutchfield's Trussville Telephone Company after Crutchfield moved to Trussville in 1931. Crutchfield had already owned a telephone business in Reform, Alabama, but he moved to take a job with Southern Bell. After his arrival, several Trussville residents encouraged him to start a local telephone company. There were then only two telephone hookups in Trussville, both connected to Southern Bell: one was at Ralph Stevens's gas station, which later had the phone number "1"; the other was assigned to Dr. Thomas Wheeler, a local physician, whose phone number became "2." In 1938, after the Cahaba Project was built, Crutchfield, in the photograph below, constructed a brick house facing Magnolia Court. The family occupied the house, with a room set aside for telephone equipment and workspace. A pay phone inside the front door was available for use by those lacking home phone service. (Both courtesy of the Crutchfield family.)

Running a local telephone company was a family enterprise. Tom Jr. remembers his sisters serving time at the switchboard as early as the age of five. Shown here are, from left to right, T.O., Tom Jr., Irene, Barbara, and Betty Crutchfield and cousins Melba Jean, Velvie, and Paul Earwood. The Earwoods, who owned a nursery, took care of landscaping. (Courtesy of the Crutchfield family.)

Operators like Armatine Pullen, shown here, worked at a switchboard, placing calls locally and outside the Trussville company. Even dialing Birmingham was considered a long-distance call. In addition to providing a link between customer calls, operators often reported fires to authorities and tracked down doctors when they were making house calls. (Courtesy of the Crutchfield family.)

Lt. James Kirksey Davis (left) and Lt. Joe Amrhein pose in front of the famous B-17 *Memphis Belle*, which they used for training—the training worked. In September 1944, piloting another B-17 over Ludwigshafen, Germany, Davis lost two engines. Running low on fuel, he bombed the target, managed to reach friendly territory, and bailed out after his crew. For that mission, he received the Distinguished Flying Cross. (Courtesy of the Davis family.)

Dorothy Covington was taking a Sunday stroll in Avonwood one day when J.K. Davis, still a man of action even though the war was over, drove by on his way home. Spotting the lovely Dot, he stopped and invited her to church—she accepted. They are seen here soon after their marriage in 1947. They moved to the Project in 1948. (Courtesy of the Davis family.)

After moving to the Project, Dot kept busy with the Davis home and children's activities. J.K. was on the Trussville Utilities board, later serving it for 18 years as general manager after retiring from South Central Bell. The Trussville Chamber of Commerce awarded him its 1993 Gatekeeper Award for community service. Pictured here in the 1950s are, from left to right, Pam, Bob, Dot, and Kirk. (Courtesy of the Davis family.)

The Davises have always been a close-knit family. All four Davis siblings pose here several years ago on the West Mall, near their childhood home. They are, from left to right, Pam Davis Hodge, Bob Davis, Carol Davis McKelvey, and Kirk Davis. Kirk died in 1998. Dot has lived in the same two-story house for 60 years. Bob and his wife, Leslie, live next door, and two of their sons live in West Mall duplexes. (Courtesy of the Davis family.)

Young John Lee Garrison met Irene Florence Turner when her family moved to Trussville. To say she caught his eye would probably be an understatement. And, Irene evidently felt the same way about him. They courted for a while, and then at age 17 they decided to get married. They knew their parents would not approve, so they eloped, returning to their respective homes until they could figure out a way to break the news to their families. This arrangement lasted for several months before Irene worked up the courage to tell her mother. Though the news was a shock, the parents quickly adjusted. Irene's father even offered Garrison a job in his automotive body–repair business in East Lake. The Garrisons remained in Trussville, raising four children in the Cahaba Project. Known as a bit of a prankster, John was serious when it came to civic duty. He was a 32nd degree Mason, a member of the Lions Club, and a three-term Trussville city councilman. (Courtesy of the Garrison family.)

Lester Tucker and Eloise Jordan often courted in the front yard of the Jordan home on Meadow Lane. Eloise's parents, Eva and Matthew Dawson Jordan, were among the original residents of the Cahaba Project. Lester's parents, Pierce and Velma Tucker, lived on Main Street, later moving to the Project to escape increasing downtown traffic. Lester and Eloise married on June 5, 1942, and had two children, Lester Jr. and Susan. (Courtesy of Matt and Aleicia Hornsby.)

Rumor had it that George and Jean Glenn stayed up all night packing the day before the Cahaba Project homes were made available to renters. The young couple wanted to be the first to move in. They were also the first of the Project families to welcome a new baby. The first of their five children, George Glenn Jr. (seen here with Jean), was born on August 8, 1938. (Courtesy of Tandi Glenn Smith.)

Not long after his parents moved into the Cahaba Project, Ralph Mitchell Jr. was one of the many postwar boomer babies to put in an appearance. Here, he poses as a Christmas gift in the living room of the Mitchells' Rockridge Avenue home. (Courtesy of Ralph and Sheree Mitchell.)

Ralph Sr. and Etta Mae Mitchell were among the many young couples to move to Trussville after World War II courtesy of the GI Bill. In 1957, daughter Camille was born with a heart defect and, at age eight, traveled with her mother and a neighbor to the Mayo Clinic for corrective surgery. To pay for the procedure, the Trussville Volunteer Fire Department organized a community fundraising effort. Sadly, Camille survived only briefly following the surgery. (Courtesy of Ralph and Sheree Mitchell.)

Emory and Etta McCrory and their four children—Mary Louise, Carl Joe, Jerry, and Betty Jean—lived just a couple of blocks off Main Street. Their home on Maple Avenue was in old Trussville before the town and the Cahaba Project became one entity in 1947. (Courtesy of the Sims family.)

This photograph of Mary Louise McCrory was taken at the Cahaba Project's stone gazebo, located at the corner of Main Street and Parkway Drive. Over the years, the gazebo has proven a popular backdrop for photographers and their subjects, as well as a one of the city's most recognizable landmarks. (Courtesy of the Sims family.)

Etta McCrory (right) and daughter Mary Louise enjoy some time playing in the snow, a rare treat in the normally mild climate of central Alabama. For all his good looks, barely visible corncob pipe, and fashionable head wear, the poor snowman likely lasted only a few days before melting away. (Courtesy of the Sims family.)

Pretty and popular Mary Louise McCrory married handsome Bill Sims in 1950. Though she left her parents' home, she did not move far away. The couple's home on Birch Street was directly behind the McCrorys' home on Maple Avenue. Bill and Mary Louise had two children, Mike and Pat, both Hewitt-Trussville High School graduates and residents of Trussville today. (Courtesy of the Sims family.)

Some of the Sims cousins' favorite and most frequent playmates were each other. In these photographs, they spend a little time, for whatever reason, in a "no dumping" zone. In the photograph at right are Mike (left) and Tommy; below are Pat (left) and Diane. "The majority of all my first cousins have stayed right here around Trussville, where we grew up together playing and fussing and fighting and playing some more," says Mike. "While we might have sometimes fussed among ourselves, no one else had better mess with any one of us if they did not want the whole Sims clan of cousins after them." (Both courtesy of the Sims family.)

Nothing was more fun for the grandchildren of Sam and Ruby Sims than to gather with the rest of the family at the home of "Papaw" and "Mamaw" for Sunday dinner. After a traditional Southern potluck meal that naturally included fried chicken and banana pudding—and maybe a few hotdogs for the kids—the adults would sit on the big front porch and watch the kids play softball or kickball. "We always liked it best when my dad and some of his brothers would play the outfielders for us, shagging balls when one of us could actually hit one all the way to the outfield," Mike Sims recalls. "Then they would fumble the ball around, dropping it or overthrowing it so the little ones had time to make a home run, too." Sam (far left) and Ruby (far right) lived on Pop Stone Circle in the Roper Station area, a few miles south of downtown Trussville. Ancestor Elijah Sims moved to the area from South Carolina in 1823. (Courtesy of the Sims family.)

Four

A COMMUNITY OF FAITH

Pioneers settling in central Alabama realized the importance of both education and faith. This artist's rendering shows the Cahawba Meeting House, a one-room log structure that doubled as a school and meetinghouse. Most settlers were either Baptists or Methodists, and the two denominations used the cabin on alternate Sundays. The building also provided space for quilting bees, cornhuskings, and other events. (Courtesy of First Baptist Church Trussville.)

On July 14, 1821, nine men and women who had brought their Baptist heritage to the Alabama frontier met to organize the Cahawba Baptist Church under the leadership of Elder Sion Blythe. Today's First Baptist Church descends from that small group of believers. This artist's rendering of that church shows a modest log structure resembling the homes of the congregation. During the 1820s and 1830s, more people became affiliated with Cahawba Baptist, and the little church grew. After a bloody Civil War and the expansion of railroads and industrial development in boomtown Birmingham, Cahawba Baptist moved to a new home, mainly to escape the clatter of nearby rail lines. The name was then changed to Trussville Baptist Church. A cemetery and historical marker located on Main Street in downtown Trussville mark the site of this church. (Courtesy of First Baptist Church Trussville.)

The Cahaba Project brought in hundreds of new residents, and the Baptist church needed to expand, but plans for a new building were postponed when World War II began. Afterward, as members returned from military service, the congregation, by then known as First Baptist, resumed its plans, with Pastor Grover C. Walker leading the way. In November 1946, the church moved into this sanctuary.

THIS BUILDING IS DEDICATED TO
DR. RICHARD E. FRANCIS
WHO SERVED AS PASTOR OF THE FIRST BAPTIST CHURCH FROM 1965 TO 1988.

DR. FRANCIS WAS A STRONG LEADER, A DEDICATED WORKER, AND A COMPASSIONATE FRIEND. TAKEN FROM THE BOOK OF PHILLIPIANS, HIS LAST CHARGE TO THIS CHURCH WAS, "PRESS TOWARD THE MARK FOR THE PRIZE OF THE HIGH CALLING OF GOD IN CHRIST JESUS." PHIL. 3:14.

This plaque honors Rev. Richard E. Francis, who began a 23-year ministry at First Baptist Trussville in June 1965. Infused with energy and dedication, Francis encouraged the congregation to rebuild, and in 1967 the church dedicated a new sanctuary. A bell tower and Christian life center further expanded church facilities during the 1970s. Francis was still providing strong spiritual leadership at his death in 1988. (Courtesy of First Baptist Church Trussville.)

Like the Baptists, Methodist worshippers used the meetinghouse for several years. In 1867, they built a church with a tall steeple equipped with a bell to summon worshippers. Dedicated lay members kept the church going. One was Perry Bluford Wilson, the Sunday school superintendent for 53 years, who often also served as secretary-treasurer. Shown here are the Wilsons' son John Wesley Wilson and his wife, May Ransom Day. (Courtesy of First United Methodist of Trussville.)

Methodist women have traditionally gathered together to pray, work on mission projects, and socialize. This turn-of-the-century photograph shows a group of Trussville Methodist ladies at a watermelon cutting. (Courtesy of First United Methodist of Trussville.)

In 1937, First Methodist negotiated with the Jefferson County Board of Education to exchange church property for school property across the road, including Trussville Grammar School. So, the white school building became a church, and the old church property was part of the land on which a new school was built. Renovations turned the old building, shown here, into a house of worship. Over the next two decades, the church made more improvements.

A new Methodist facility was constructed on the same campus as the renovated school. The first project was an educational building, completed in 1954. The next step was a new sanctuary, constructed at a cost of $160,000 and completed in 1960. A number of renovations and improvements have been made since to better serve the congregation and community.

Even though construction had begun only a few months before, the new First Methodist sanctuary was completed in time for the 1960 Easter Sunday service. Since then, the location of the church has remained the same, but additions to buildings and church programs and renovations have been made over the years as the congregation has grown. (Courtesy of First United Methodist of Trussville.)

Mt. Joy Baptist Church, built by and for slaves in 1857, is still a viable part of Trussville's African American community. Mt. Joy is the oldest slave-founded church in Jefferson County. With a membership of about 200, the Mt. Joy congregation merged with that of Mt. Canaan, another African American congregation, in 2000. Earlier Mt. Joy buildings have been razed, but an older Mt. Canaan church is shown here. (Courtesy of Mt. Joy Baptist Church.)

A marquee message welcomes worshippers to a late-20th-century version of Mt. Joy Baptist Church. Completed in 1998, the construction of this sanctuary brought about the re-unification of the Mt. Joy and Mt. Canaan congregations, because during that time, the two groups worshipped together and were led by the same pastor. Growth was rapid, and in 2007 another sanctuary accommodating more worshippers was built to replace the church. (Courtesy of Mt. Joy Baptist Church.)

Only this marker is left to indicate the former location of New Bethel Baptist Church. The church was founded in the early 1900s, when the Trussville blast furnace was still in operation, employing a number of African American workers. When New Bethel closed in 1999, many members moved to Mt. Joy. (Courtesy of Mt. Joy Baptist Church.)

Mt. Joy had a long and proud history when Rev. Larry Hollman assumed the pastorate in 1992, but membership and attendance were dwindling. During his pastorate, the church has experienced tremendous growth, and the old, outdated church building was torn down. Hollman also has been instrumental in uniting all three area African American congregations into one. (Courtesy of Mt. Joy Baptist Church.)

The seeds that grew into Holy Infant of Prague Catholic Church were planted in 1939, when Fr. John A. Bratton began celebrating Mass twice a month in a vacant apartment in the newly completed Cahaba Project. After a 1940 census of Trussville showed 50 Catholic families in the surrounding areas, the need for a church for area residents of the Catholic faith became clear. So, the following year, Bishop T.J. Toolen appointed Fr. Frank Giri as the first pastor for the area, and preparations for building a church began. With an initial donation of $5,000 made by prominent preacher and broadcaster Msgr. (later Archbishop) Fulton J. Sheen, land was purchased on Hewitt Street, and Sheen chose the name Holy Infant of Prague. Ground was broken for the building project on August 31, 1941. This photograph shows church leaders participating in the ceremony. (Courtesy of Holy Infant of Prague Catholic Church.)

Work on the new Holy Infant sanctuary, designed to seat 100 people, got under way in October 1941, just before the United States's entry into World War II curtailed many building projects. Workers completed construction in February 1942. Parishioners had been involved in installing plumbing, statues, pews, and a life-sized crucifix, and the Gallagher family of New Jersey donated interior furnishings. On May 10, 1942, Rev. T.J. Toolen, the bishop of Mobile, led the dedication of the church before an overflow crowd of dignitaries, members, and guests. The church remained a mission parish until 1947, when it was raised to the rank of a parish, with Rev. Joseph Adams as its first resident pastor. The population of the Trussville area expanded so rapidly during the 1980s that the church added sanctuary and classroom space in 1991 to accommodate needs accompanying that growth. This photograph shows a partial view of the expanded church as it was during the last part of the 20th century. (Courtesy of Holy Infant of Prague Catholic Church.)

In 1948, a rectory, seen above, was erected adjoining the church lot. A more up-to-date brick rectory was constructed later at another location to make room for needed church expansion. This included a sanctuary seating 250 people and four additional classrooms. By the turn of the 21st century, the church again was too small for its growing congregation. The diocese sold the Hewitt Street property, and the church moved to a location on Highway 11, where a new parish complex was constructed. The first Sunday mass was held September 30, 2006. The photograph below shows the new Holy Infant church and site. (Courtesy of Holy Infant of Prague Catholic Church.)

A small group of Episcopalians organized a Trussville congregation in 1942, meeting in various places. After 13 years without a church home, members of Holy Cross pitched in to construct a long-anticipated worship center. Used bricks were donated for that first construction, and parishioners, including John Alexander (seen here) spent hours cleaning them by hand. The worship center and adjoining rooms were completed in time to hold a 1955 Christmas Eve service. (Courtesy of Holy Cross Episcopal Church.)

With a permanent structure in an area that was ripe for growth, Holy Cross needed full-time leadership. For years, the church shared the services of ministers with other small churches, but in 1980 the Reverend Ron DelBene began serving as full-time rector. The next rector, the Reverend Stephen Rottgers, spearheaded the development of TEAM (Trussville Ecumenical Assistive Ministry), an organization of local churches that provides food, clothing, and other assistance to needy families in the area. (Courtesy of Holy Cross Episcopal Church.)

The year 1941 was a pivotal one for the United States as well as for the world. America was still emerging from the Great Depression and was on the brink of World War II. By year's end, many Trussville men would be called to active military duty. The spiritual renaissance that affected the rest of the country also touched the area, and a group of believers on the south side of town formed a church. Beginning with a "brush arbor," the congregation later built a permanent structure, seen in the 1951 photograph below. As the church initially had no running water, baptisms took place in a nearby creek. The photograph above shows Brother Arthur Tillman, a country preacher who had become the church pastor in 1942, baptizing new believers. Tillman also was known for performing marriage ceremonies and, according to legend, on one occasion he stopped plowing and married a couple in his cornfield. The church became Trussville Southside Baptist Church. Today, it occupies a modern brick building and has about 150 worshippers. (Both courtesy of Ann Bradford Billingsley.)

Founded in 1865 as Cave Springs Congregational First Cumberland Church, this church was named for the springs and caves at the rear of the church property. The presbytery soon changed the name to Mt. Nebo Presbyterian Church, the name it bore when this two-story white building was dedicated in May 1890. The historic cemetery across Highway 11 has retained the Mt. Nebo name. The church's name was changed again in 1958, this time to First Presbyterian Church of Trussville. During the 1960s, members installed memorial windows and converted the building into a one-story structure.

The Trussville Church of Christ was organized in 1942, but it did not complete and move into this concrete-block house of worship until 1947. Until then, the congregants used the Trussville First Presbyterian Church as a house of worship. Since then, this building has been remodeled extensively and has been updated with a brick exterior.

Five

GETTING DOWN TO BUSINESS

This cluttered sign on Highway 11 near downtown Trussville once greeted visitors and welcomed weary commuters home from their Birmingham jobs. It not only served as a symbol of the hospitality the city is known for, but it was also an indication of the city's abundance of civic pride, strong business community, and faith-based family values.

These civic-minded individuals composed Trussville's first city council, which served from July 1947 until 1952. Shown here are, from left to right, Richard Beard, Mary Lou Farley, Horace Norrell, George Glenn, J. Alton Williams, and John Yarbrough. Williams was president of the Cahaba Civic Association (CCA) and a member of the committee responsible for "forming a plan of incorporation and operation of a city government to serve both Cahaba and Trussville," according to the August 1946 minutes of the association. Prior to incorporation, the Cahaba Project was considered a separate community from Trussville. Norrell served as mayor until 1960, and Yarbrough was mayor for the 1964–1968 term. Williams was elected mayor in 1972, also serving one term. Outside of their council duties, the four councilmen (or "aldermen" as they were called in those days) were all hardworking businessmen. But, Mrs. Farley had the toughest job of all; for many years, she was principal of Hewitt Elementary. (Courtesy of Trussville Historical Archives.)

Trussville's first city hall (above) was a building on Main Street owned by Matthew F. Roper. The jail was located behind the building. City offices were subsequently moved to a building on South Chalkville Road (below), constructed by William Towers in 1949 and leased to the Town of Trussville for $100 a month for 144 months. Today's city hall, completed in 1959, started out as a single 15,012 square-foot facility that cost approximately $225,000 to build. It has since expanded into a complex of buildings that house not only government offices, but the main police and fire stations, public works, and Trussville Utilities.

Trussville's first police car, which began patrolling in 1947, was actually a regular truck painted by Trussville's first police chief, Joe B. Vann. When the city was formed, Vann and A.E. Quick were the only two police officers on duty. In contrast, today's police force has 64 members and specialized vehicles custom-fit for law enforcement.

This 1960 photograph depicts only a small number of Trussville volunteer firefighters who have given of their time and effort over the years. While volunteer brigades often fade away as cities grow and begin hiring paid firefighters, Trussville Fire & Rescue's volunteer program continues to thrive well into the new millennium.

The Trussville Area Chamber of Commerce (TACC) was organized in 1946, but it was not until the restoration of Heritage Hall in the mid-1980s that a permanent home for the organization was established. The chamber began operating on a full-time basis out of its office on the Parkway Drive side of the building in 1988. Not only does the office provide a headquarters for the business of promoting Trussville to the outside world, it also serves as an information center for business owners and individuals seeking to relocate to Trussville. Many a community event and civic effort has been planned and executed from the chamber's Heritage Hall office, including festivals, political forums, and business-related seminars. Over the course of the TACC's existence, membership has grown from a handful of downtown Trussville businesses to well over 300 members from all over the Birmingham metro area. (Courtesy of Trussville Area Chamber of Commerce.)

Trussville's Heritage Hall was originally built to serve as the Cahaba Project's co-op store and service station. At varying times, it housed a beauty shop, a launderette, and other community conveniences. When the co-op was dissolved in the late 1940s, the building was transferred to the City of Trussville for use as a community center and library. It was later deeded to the Jefferson County Board of Education to provide space for Hewitt-Trussville High School's band and choral programs. When a new high school was built in the early 1980s, the old co-op building reverted to the city, and in 1987 it underwent a major restoration: the former band room became the Arts Council of the Trussville Area (ACTA) Theater, the choral area became a historical museum and meeting room, and the filling station wing became the offices of the Trussville Area Chamber of Commerce. (Courtesy of Trussville Area Chamber of Commerce.)

Trussville Train Station 1950's

When the railroad came to Trussville in the late 1800s, it brought regular mail service, freight shipments, and passenger service. In the 1960s, it provided transportation for elementary school kids to the Birmingham Zoo. "It was wonderful, the greatest thing ever," recalls Carla Lane McKenzie, "and it was truly a sad time when the train stopped running." The Trussville train station is seen here in the 1950s.

This plain but functional structure on Main Street served as the Trussville branch of the US Post Office from 1950 until 1980. Built by Sam Liles, it has since proven an excellent location for retail sales, specifically for home decor and gifts. One of the three boutiques housed there over the years was appropriately named The Olde Post Office.

These busy workingwomen served as operators for the Trussville Telephone Company. Not only were they responsible for operating the switchboard, they sounded the fire alarm, provided local residents with the correct time, and served as the town doctor's answering service. At one time, only two lines connected Trussville callers to Birmingham; thus, phoning someone in the "big city" often meant waiting one's turn to be put through.

This redbrick building on Chalkville Road was constructed in 1958 to accommodate the equipment required for Trussville's first telephone dial system. Regardless of the newfangled apparatus, many local residents had party lines well into the 1960s. Today's Trussville phone system is much more sophisticated, but its modern conveniences can never quite equal the illicit thrill of listening in on the neighbors' phone calls.

These mid-20th-century street scenes depict a different—and smaller—town than the Trussville of today. The building that once housed Norrell's Dixie Super Store (above, far right) is now a Dollar General Store. The multi-business building next door was long ago demolished to make way for a post office and retail parking area. Norrell's connected on the other side with T.E. Glenn Department Store, which for many years stood on the northwest corner of Main Street and Chalkville Road. Farther north on the same side of Main Street were Trussville Cleaners and the Gulf and Standard Oil stations (below). Beyond those stood the Glendale Mills building, most recently occupied by a discount furniture store. (Both courtesy of Trussville Utilities.)

In the years before interstate highways, US Highway 11 was the primary route from New Orleans to Birmingham. The road then wound northeastward through cities like Chattanooga, Roanoke, and Harrisburg, all the way to upstate New York and its border with Canada; thus did the part of Highway 11 that runs through Trussville once teem with traffic from parts north and south, making the sleepy town a prime spot for a variety of service stations and garages. Local entrepreneur William "Bill" Towers owned one such establishment. Towers Gulf Service, a handy, all-purpose stop for travelers as well as locals, offered not only a full-service fuel stop for their cars but food for their bodies as well. Towers's sister Evelyn Venable ran a popular café at the station called The Good Eats Shop from 1936 to 1941. The restaurant later became the Kenwood Café, bought and run by Bertha Kenyon and Muriel Woodman.

One of the longest-lived businesses in the history of Trussville, Mabe Garage went from being a downtown roadside wrecker and repair business in 1921 to a sizable lawn and garden equipment dealership in its latter years. To eliminate confusion as to the nature of Mabe's services, the name of the business was changed in 1990 from Mabe Garage and Lawnmower Repair to Mabe Power Equipment Center. A devastating flood in downtown Trussville in 2003 and three years of drought during the next few years took a huge toll. After 91 years in business and three generations of family ownership, Mabe closed its doors for the final time in 2012.

Other automobile-related businesses on Trussville's Main Street over the years included Stephens Garage (right), a Texaco station built by Ralph Stephens in 1938, and Ted Martin Garage (below), a Shell Oil station. Stephens was located on the south side of Main Street, less than a block east of Chalkville Road (the present-day Regions Bank location). Martin Garage was located across the street. Ted Martin eventually had his old, redbrick building torn down and replaced with a new, modern-looking facility. Sometime after World War II, he became a Gulf Oil dealer and remained so until his retirement. Mayor Gene Melton worked part-time for Martin's Gulf station between 1963 and 1966 while attending Hewitt-Trussville High School.

The College Drive In and Shell station, built by Enos Vann, provided customers with one-stop service: they could fill up their tanks and grab a quick bite to eat at the same time. The owner was a descendant of some of Trussville's earliest settlers, who came to Alabama from North Carolina in the 1820s.

While the name does not sound all that savory, Hooker's Café, by all accounts, was a good and reasonably priced place to get a bite to eat. Owned by W. Floyd Hooker, the café offered a "Special Cook's Night Out Steak Dinner" for 50¢. After the restaurant closed, the c. 1928 building was remodeled to accommodate a beauty shop and a dry-cleaning business.

The Bama Drive In on Main Street had several owners over the many years it remained in business, but, recalls Pat Sims Tillman, it was always "a great place to eat. They had the best hamburger steaks." A favorite eating-out choice for people of all ages, the Bama served not only as a hangout for local high school kids, it was a family restaurant at dinnertime as well as a convenient place to catch a bite of breakfast and a cup or two of coffee on a Saturday morning. In addition to those tasty hamburger steaks, the Bama Drive In menu included hamburgers, cheeseburgers, barbecue sandwiches, hot dogs, malts, and shakes—all at reasonable prices. In the mid-1950s, a T-bone steak could be purchased for well under $2. Back then, a family of four could conceivably dine for under $10, including some of the Bama's signature fried pies for dessert.

In the 1950s, teenage boys often took their girlfriends to the Bama Drive In for a bite to eat. Carhops came out to take orders and then delivered the goods on a tray designed to hang from the car window. In the photograph at left, Juanalda Simmons and Joe Curl strike an affectionate pose in front of the Bama's outdoor menu sign. Prominently listed at the bottom of the billboard are the famous Bama homemade fried pies, later sold in places like McDonald's and Jack's. The pastries were such a hit that a separate facility was built nearby to make fried pies. That building now houses the Chocolate Biscuit Tearoom.

George Glenn was the ultimate small-town entrepreneur and the owner of several businesses around town, but he was also a contributing member of the Trussville community. Glenn served as an alderman on the first town council after Trussville was incorporated in 1947. He also served as a volunteer fireman for a number of years. One of the original residents of the Cahaba Project, Glenn and his wife, Jean, were the first to move into the Project, later becoming the parents of the first baby born to a family there (see page 49). Several of the Glenn children and grandchildren remain residents of and are active in the Trussville community to this day.

George Glenn built his first Sinclair station on Main Street in 1936. In addition to gasoline, he sold coal and ice and provided hauling services. There was also the entertainment factor: the outdoor car hoist (above, right center) was a source of fascination for kids throughout the community. The service station's success begat another successful business, when Glenn was compelled to build a separate facility for the growing ice business a few years later (see page 88). The station was replaced by a more modern version when a shiny new Glenn's Sinclair (below) opened about two and a half decades after the first one.

Much ado accompanied the opening of the new Sinclair station. Above, George Glenn poses in front of the upgraded, relocated business for an advertising photograph. The full-service establishment's products included oil, tires, and a refreshing cold drink from a now-vintage Coca-Cola machine. Below, a vertical banner promises a "Grand Opening Soon." The photograph shows a row of Glenn-owned properties, including the Sinclair station, the Trussville Icehouse, and the former location of Glenn Service Station, lining an entire downtown block on the south side of Main Street. The three buildings, although no longer occupied by the original businesses, remain standing in downtown Trussville.

The Trussville Icehouse, built by Joe Massey, Earl Melton, and Jack Box for George Glenn in 1949, sold block and crushed ice to individuals and businesses. Many a freezer of homemade ice cream was churned with the aid of the icehouse's product. Over the years, various young men loaded and hauled bags of ice all over the Birmingham area. The late-1960s photograph below shows Darrell Harper (left) and the owner's son, Bobby Glenn, getting ready to make rounds. "My grandfather used to send me with them when I was nine or ten to help deliver bags of ice," recalls the oldest of the seven Glenn grandchildren, Steve Glenn. "My job was to count them."

Thomas Hunter's Trussville Drug Store suffered heavy fire damage in 1938. In those days, firefighting capabilities were limited, as Trussville had yet to organize an official department and purchase a fire engine. Today's fire department consists of a highly trained combination of paid and volunteer personnel equipped with the latest in transportation and technology.

Trussville Drug Store, on the northeast corner of Main Street and Chalkville Road, shared space with Dr. W.D. Thompson, the only physician in town for many years. The lot on which this building still stands was once occupied by a store owned by prominent businessman Dyer N. Talley. In its time, the Talley store was the largest building in Trussville, with a reported 100,000 bricks in its walls.

Norrell's, the first full-fledged supermarket in town, was a great place for mothers to shop. Not only was it convenient, the kids liked it, too. Barri Gabert Harrison recalls going there with her mother, Peggy: "There was a big magazine rack by the front door, and I would look at magazines until mother was through shopping. Then, if I was really lucky, she would buy me one of Norrell's wonderful hotdogs!"

Pam Bell Bagley said, "I used to walk up to Mr. Jones's store quite often. I remember that if I walked in during the Jones's lunch or dinner, he would tell me to help myself, that he'd be with me in a few minutes. I never thought a thing about it. Mr. Jones also would tell me that I could spend the change on candy, my mama wouldn't mind. But I never did. I knew she would!"

This interior photograph of Western Auto shows the wide array of merchandise available to Trussville shoppers in the 1950s and 1960s. Owned and managed by J.W. Davis, the store was known for such brands as Western Flyer bicycles, Citation appliances, and Wizard tools. It served its Main Street customers well. "I bought my first shotgun there for $60," recalls Ralph Mitchell, "and I've still got it."

Prater Rexall Drugs on Chalkville Road was known not only for its friendly hometown service, but it also had one of the best soda fountains around. In addition to medication and other health-related products, the store carried a selection of toys, gifts, and sundries. A well-stocked candy counter made the store a popular after-school stop for kids attending the nearby Hewitt Elementary School.

The Mann brothers, Sedric and F.W. (nicknamed "Boy"), opened the car lot pictured above on Main Street in 1963. They later sold it to Berford Brown, who renamed it Trussville Motors. In the meantime, another business they started in 1953 was thriving. Mann Bros. Metal Plating re-chromed and resold car and truck bumpers and other chrome pieces that had rusted or otherwise been damaged. "Uncle Sedric knew chemistry, and my dad had welding and mechanical skills," recalls Boy's son, Thomas Mann. "They were a good team." The company remained in business until the late 1980s, although both brothers had died by then. It was then sold to Southeastern Bumper and later to an Arkansas company. It closed in the early 1990s.

Only a few times over the years has downtown Trussville experienced significant flooding, and this photograph depicts one of those instances. The exact year of this flood is unknown, but according to the model of the car it appears to have occurred sometime in the 1950s. A similar flood took the downtown area by surprise in the spring of 2003, and the effects were devastating. Nearly 10 inches of rain fell in the span of only four hours, flooding the Trussville Municipal Complex, putting city records at risk, and submerging city vehicles. A few miles up the road, a mud slide blocked the entrance to Camp Coleman. Since then, steps have been taken and future upgrades are planned to reduce the chances of another incident taking a damaging toll on local homes and businesses.

Any small town worth its salt in the 1940s and 1950s had a movie theater. While the Trussville Theatre on the south side of Main Street lacked bright lights and a fancy marquee, it drew the local cinematic crowd like moths to a flame. And, it provided entertainment at what even back then was a bargain price. Most of today's moviegoers have only heard of a time when a Saturday matinee cost only a few cents. "We could see a feature, a news reel, a serial like *Tarzan* or *The King of the Royal Mounted*, a cartoon, and a second feature," recalls George Bacon. "Saturday night features would start around 7:30 p.m. and cost 35¢ for adults and 10¢ for children. Of course you could buy popcorn and candy, too." With a little extra cash to spend, a kid could easily get a haircut after a morning at the movies. Reuben King's barbershop was conveniently located next door.

Six

EDUCATION
AND RECREATION

In 1869, Birmingham native and Civil War veteran Robert Green Hewitt founded Trussville Academy. After teaching for several years, he was twice elected tax collector for Jefferson County. He was appointed county superintendent of education but declined the appointment. Hewitt later served as president of the Jefferson County Board of Education. In 1925, Trussville's R.G. Hewitt School was named in his honor. (Courtesy of Birmingham, Alabama, Public Library Archives.)

This clapboard building served as Trussville Grammar School from 1903 until 1938. Prior to its construction, local students attended Trussville Academy, a modest-sized, aging structure situated somewhere off South Chalkville Road near the railroad tracks. Students began the 1903 school year in the old academy building, moving to the new school a few months later.

A school for higher grades was built across from the old Trussville Grammar School in 1922. Classrooms were added three years later to make Trussville School a senior high school, and the name was changed to R.G. Hewitt School. The first senior class graduated on May 25, 1927, Professor Hewitt's birthday.

Many a class posed for group photographs on the front steps of R.G. Hewitt School, which later became Hewitt Elementary. This generally solemn group differed from later classes in their style of dress. No matter the age or era, though, as the familiar backdrop of white, wooden-paned windows was always the same.

Decades later, these smiling fourth graders strike their own poses in front of the old school. Though they do not look much different from today's fourth graders, the open window on the left tells of a time gone by, when air-conditioned comfort was not yet the norm in school buildings. (Courtesy of Jimmie Morrow King.)

Initial plans for the Cahaba Project called for a community building, with extras rooms to be used as classrooms if needed. Planners soon realized, however, that without another educational facility, Trussville's schools would be overloaded with the influx of new families. So, the plan was flip-flopped: a new school with extra rooms for community activities would be erected. In June 1936, the US government entered into an agreement with the Jefferson County Board of

Education to build a new school in line with the Resettlement Administration's plan to furnish educational opportunities to children of Trussville and surrounding areas. The board originally intended for the new school to house grades one through nine, with senior grades remaining at the old school. Again, plans changed, and Hewitt High School opened with grades 10 through 12 in the fall of 1938. (Courtesy of Ron Burkett.)

Young Beatrice Anderson could hardly contain her excitement about attending the new Hewitt High School. She was the first to arrive on opening day. To commemorate the occasion, a teacher snapped this photograph of Bea waiting on the front porch for school officials to unlock the building. (Courtesy of Jerry Wilson.)

A popular place for community gatherings during the early days of the Cahaba Project was the gymnasium of Hewitt High School. When not being used for high school basketball and other sports, the gym became an auditorium where movies, plays, concerts, dances, and other entertainment or social events took place. (Courtesy of Jim Robinson.)

In September 1937, the Jefferson County Board of Education worked out an even trade with Trussville Methodist Church: the Trussville Grammar School property was swapped for a parcel of land adjacent to the R.G. Hewitt School. This gave the school a larger expanse of land and the Methodists a larger, newer building.

The Hewitt High School class of 1945 had 29 graduates. In contrast, recent graduating classes at today's Hewitt-Trussville High School exceed 300. The difference becomes even greater when one considers that in 1945, Trussville schools were drawing students from all over the northeast part of Jefferson County. Today's Trussville schools serve only students living within Trussville city limits.

Dot Robinson, an inveterate amateur photographer, did not hesitate to tackle group shots, even when they involved a bunch of squirming kids. Here, she has captured son Jimmy's 1948–1949 second-grade class at Hewitt Grammar School. Jimmy is third from the right in the second row. The children's teacher, Mrs. McLain, is in the back, at left. (Courtesy of Jim Robinson.)

Sixth-grade boys often get into trouble, and Jimmy was no different. This scolding by his teacher, Mrs. Brown, took place on the front porch of Hewitt Elementary. Unfortunately for him, the photographer capturing the scene was his mother. Talking himself back into his mother's good graces likely helped Jim prepare for his future in local politics. He was a two-term Trussville city councilman. (Courtesy of Jim Robinson.)

This moment of prayer took place in the mid-1940s in the Hewitt High School auditorium, which also served as the gymnasium. Though the exact reason for the prayer time is long forgotten, the seriousness of the moment is clear. It could have been a prayer for soldiers still fighting World War II overseas, or it could have been a routine assembly. Regardless of the reason, each person in the room is a study in reverence. Every head is bowed, and every eye is closed. In the years since this photograph was taken, public prayer in school settings has been discouraged and even legislated against; however, it does not mean it never happens. It has often been said that as long as teachers continue to give pop quizzes and final exams, there will always be prayer in schools. (Courtesy of the Sims family.)

Mary Louise McCrory, who only months later would become Mrs. Bill Sims, was named the first Miss Trussville at the town's Fourth of July celebration in 1949. In honor of her selection as the local beauty queen, Mayor Horace Norrell presented her with the loving cup she clutches in the photograph at left. Donated by A&A Ash Jewelry Company of Birmingham, the trophy remains a treasured memento in the Sims family. The photograph below shows McCrory (fifth from left) and her fellow contestants prior to the announcement of the winner. The lack of smiles could likely be attributed to a combination of long dresses and midsummer heat. (Both courtesy of the Sims family.)

HEWITT HI-LIGHT

VOL. 3   MARCH, 1945   No. 1

Chatterbox
I. C. All

Seems like we're having another contest at Hewitt. The contestants are Millie Tucker and Doris McMichael. The prize is Hoyt Todd.

* * *

Seems as though Ed Coleman has some competition around here. How about that Bill Hart?

* * *

We hear that Donald Grauer and Hugh have been going to Brentwood for tea. What do you know about this Gloria Turner?

* * *

The tide has turned for Charlsie Lee and Jack Goodwin. Seems like Charlsie has her eye on another man.

* * *

Notice! Anyone finding a loose boy friend please bring to Francis Trull, who is still hunting one.

* * *

Have you heard Earl S. sing. No? You lucky thing.

* * *

Wanted: One man, tall or short, fat or skinney, rich or poor, hair or toupee, just so he's a man. Apply Anne Harding.

* * *

Billy McClelland, a certain girl has been saying sweet things about

Nominees For Miss Valentine

(Left to right)—Jean Bonner, Josephine Walden, Gloria Turner, Doris Self (second place), Lurline Whitworth (Miss Valentine), Bernice Williams (third place), Shellie Templeton, Sue Goodwin, and Claire Williams.

VALENTINE QUEEN ELECTED

Valentine day found Hewitt in an uproar, trying to decide or

HEWITT RATES HIGH IN VISUAL EDUCATION

Two thirds of all learning is accomplished through vision. Educators agree that a well balanced visual education program is invaluable in the modern program.

Hewitt High School began its visual education program eight years ago. Benefits derived by this program cannot be estimated. Every department in the school has profited by the films shown. This year 120 films have been booked, covering every subject taught. Films on History, Science, Home Economics, Health, English, Business, Physical Education, Shop and Social Studies are included in the bookings. Every teacher is given an opportunity of selecting films for each of their classes. Each class in school averages four films during the year. That gives the individual pupil an average of two educational films a month.

We book most of our films from Y. M. C. A. Motion Picture Bureau, Dallas, Texas, University Film Library, University, Alabama, and Jefferson County Film Library. The films run low in cost from 50 cents to 4.50 per film. Many of the most beneficial of the films come to us free—often with

---

In true World War II–era fashion, the banner of this March 1945 issue of the *Hewitt Hi-Light* newspaper urges readers to "Do Your Part" and "Buy Bonds and Stamps." The gossip column on the left takes a more whimsical turn. The article on the right, however, reveals that Hewitt was an exceptional school, rating high in visual education. Using what was state-of-the-art equipment—a 16-millimeter projector and a beaded glass screen—teachers were able to show educational films to their classes for very little cost. In addition to the learning value of the films, student operators gained valuable experience. After assisting with the school's program, one student operator, the article stated, wound up landing a job in commercial entertainment. Films shown during the 1944–1945 school year were *The Monroe Doctrine, Championship Typing, Meat and Romance, Survival of the Fittest,* and *Man Without a Country.* (Courtesy of the Garrison family.)

Participation in the fine arts has long played an important role in the education of Trussville students. While art classes have always been popular electives, the choral and band programs provide choices for students wishing to express themselves musically. Here, the 1947–1948 Hewitt High School Girls' Glee Club, directed by Birdye Faircloth, poses for a pre-performance photograph on the stage of the school auditorium. Hewitt also had a strong boys' glee club that year (see page 110), and the two clubs often performed with other groups within the choral and band departments. Though most mid-20th-century American glee clubs were actually choruses in the strictest sense of the term, and in recent decades have been referred to as such, the concept of glee clubs has recently been re-popularized with the Fox Network show *Glee*. (Courtesy of Gayle Williams Glenn.)

Long before colorful flags and synchronized dance teams began dominating the field at halftime, majorettes were the undisputed stars of the show. Decked out in white boots and trim uniforms, they strutted and twirled with lively precision to the beat of the band. Here, majorettes display some off-field school spirit with black-and-gold Hewitt pennants in 1947. (Courtesy of Trussville Public Library.)

These members of the class of 1949 were but lowly freshmen. Mary Swatzell (third row, third from the right) enjoyed the unique status of having a father who moonlighted at the town theater. Alas, though, it did neither her nor her friends any good. "I never got in free," she said, regretfully. (Courtesy of Mary Louise Swatzell Kennedy.)

Chronicling the school year was (and still is) the task of the *Memento* yearbook staff—and what a task it can be. Not only are staff members compelled to become amateur photographers, experts in advertising sales, and writers and editors of copy, they have to pare things down, then pull it all together into one slim volume. Here, the 1947 *Memento* staff is hard at work. (Courtesy of Trussville Public Library.)

Working on the school newspaper often becomes the foundation for careers in editing and reporting. This rather sizable (and quite serious) group made up the 1949 staff of Hewitt's *Hi-Light* newspaper. Once described as "a scholarly paper . . . serving the best interest of our school and community," the *Hi-Light* served as predecessor to today's *Husky Howl*. (Courtesy of Trussville Public Library.)

Early on, sports became a major part of the student culture at the new Hewitt High, and within a decade the need for a stadium became clear. Built in 1949 at a cost of $40,000, this 10-acre facility became a popular venue for school activities as well as community events. Classrooms were later added underneath the stadium to accommodate a growing student population.

The 1949 Hewitt football team was the last to play without the benefit of a school stadium, but that did not stop this small but powerful group of kids from playing their hearts out for beloved coach Rufus Shelton (third row, far left). One of the tough guys on this team was junior Reuben Robison (second row, far right), future principal of the high school. (Courtesy of Trussville Public Library.)

Experts have long believed that students who participate in music programs achieve better grades and enjoy greater success later in life, and Hewitt-Trussville choir director Mary McKinnon believed that, too. "Mrs. McKinnon loved, understood, and appreciated each individual student and worked to help that individual reach maximum potential," said former student and longtime friend Gayle Glenn. "She was a leader, developing leaders, through her example and constant encouragement to be the best possible no matter what the task." McKinnon taught choral music in Trussville schools for 17 years before returning to school and ultimately becoming director of guidance and counseling services for Jefferson County Schools. (Both courtesy of Gayle Williams Glenn.)

Mary McKinnon loved nothing more than seeing the fruits of her labor as a choral teacher manifested in a full-scale musical production. The threesome in this photograph was part of the cast of the Hewitt High School Choral Department's stage version of *H.M.S. Pinafore* in 1952. A Gilbert and Sullivan opera in two acts, the story takes place aboard the British ship HMS *Pinafore*, the illusion of which was created with a panoramic ocean backdrop across the stage. With the play's comical twists and whimsical musical numbers, the Hewitt students, if this photograph is any indication, relished their roles and played them to the hilt, but not without some molding, honing, and maybe not-so-subtle direction by their diligent instructor. Other 1950s productions directed by McKinnon include *Pickles*, *The Gypsy Rover*, *In Gay Havana*, and *An Evening with Rodgers and Hammerstein*. (Courtesy of Gayle Williams Glenn.)

The 1955 school year meant changes for Hewitt High School. Not only was the name changed to Hewitt-Trussville to give the school a location-specific identification, the school colors changed from black and gold to red and gray as determined by a popular vote of the student body. In other areas, whether clubs, band, sports, football banquets, homecoming festivities, or even reading, writing, and arithmetic—all those things that fill one's high school days with enough memories and angst to last a lifetime—student life continued along as always. Most of those experiences, however, paled in comparison to the excitement of the 1955 senior prom. Here, Joan Nall and her date, Ronald Joe Moore, are gussied up for the big occasion. The prom was held that year in downtown Birmingham and featured a formal dinner and dancing. (Courtesy of Joan Nall Herren.)

Taking a break from swimming in Camp Cosby Lake during the summer of 1954 are, from left to right, Joan Nall, Martha Jo Cross, Ann Herren, Jerri Ellison, and Peggy Brown. The lake was a favorite summer meeting spot for Hewitt friends, who thought nothing of riding bicycles several miles to get together. Hewitt students came from many eastern Jefferson County communities. (Courtesy of Joan Nall Herren.)

Bill Caldwell and Joan Nall strike a pose for the 1955 edition of the Hewitt-Trussville High School yearbook, the *Memento*. Both were named Senior Favorites by their fellow students, capturing the "Best Looking" titles and earning a spot in the "Favorites" section of the annual. (Courtesy of Joan Nall Herren.)

TACKLE   WHALEY HALL   OLE MISS

After high school, Hewitt-Trussville football standout Whaley Hall crossed the west Alabama state line to play for the Ole Miss Rebels. He served as co-captain of the team in 1963 and was named the Birmingham Touchdown Club's SEC Outstanding Lineman that same year. During his college career, Hall achieved All-American status and was named a first team All-SEC tackle. He was a member of the 1962 undefeated Ole Miss team that shared national championship honors with University of Southern California and played in the 1964 Senior Bowl and Coaches Association All-America Bowl. Following his senior season, Hall was a fourth-round pick in the NFL draft by the Dallas Cowboys (number 48 overall). He was inducted into the Ole Miss Athletics Hall of Fame in 1995. (Courtesy of Ole Miss Athletics Media Relations.)

While the 1957 junior Hewitt-Trussville Huskies football team was striving for victory on the field, the pyramided group of young women (above) was cheering them on. Watching the clock and gridiron action from the sidelines was the Huskies' coach, the beloved "Piggy" Mitchell (below), who served as the HTHS head football coach from 1951 until 1963. Mitchell spent 31 of his 37 years in coaching at Jefferson County Schools and was in many ways ahead of his time in terms of high school athletics. He started dirt-court basketball leagues in schools that did not have gyms, he introduced wrestling to county schools, and he brought the T-formation offense to high schools in the Birmingham area. (Both courtesy of Trussville Public Library.)

Thanks to the efforts of several Hewitt Elementary parents, the new school library opened in 1960. The fathers built the shelves, and the mothers helped furnish the room that served as the library. Principal Mary Lou Farley can be seen in the background. (Courtesy of Paula Bradley Jones.)

Posing for photographs like this one became a yearly exercise in patience for teachers and students alike. Photographers came in, rearranged the room, and finally snapped a shot or two. Then, when all was said and done, each classroom photograph looked a lot like all the others. Nowadays, identifying classmates in these old group pictures has become a regular Facebook challenge. (Courtesy of Paula Bradley Jones.)

At some point, grades seven through nine were relocated to Hewitt High School, but by the early 1960s the nearly three-decade-old facility was bursting at the seams. So, the Jefferson County Board of Education contracted for a junior high school to be built slightly north of the high school campus, near the corner of Parkway Drive and Poplar Street. Hewitt-Trussville Junior High School opened its doors to students in grades seven and eight in 1964.

How many high school coeds can you get into a Volkswagen? At least 12 according to this 1960s photograph. While it is unlikely this crowd was able to get very far in such a tiny car, they probably had a lot of laughs trying to fit themselves into the limited space. (Courtesy of Laurie McLendon Nabors.)

Preschoolers in the 1950s and 1960s often attended Lully Wheeler's kindergarten. She started out with 10 students, using her kitchen table or front porch as the site for activities. She later renovated an old carriage house behind her home for classroom space. Kids were thrilled when the fire truck came to visit, especially when they were allowed to climb onto the back of the vehicle for a photo op. (Courtesy of Ralph and Sheree Mitchell.)

Starting in 1962, the parents of preschoolers had the option of sending their kids to the new Joyland Kindergarten at First Baptist Church Trussville. As the first director, Etta Mae Mitchell Tingle (standing, left) was compelled to be a one-woman show. She organized, scheduled, supervised, and taught the children. Her assistant in this photograph is the pastor's wife, Marjorie Holland. (Courtesy of Ralph and Sheree Mitchell.)

A midday fire on May 10, 1973, destroyed the nearly half-century-old Hewitt Elementary School. The school's files, stored in a newer brick annex next door, were spared. Other areas of the building were a total loss, including the school library and a bin of bottle caps students had been collecting over two years with the ultimate goal of seeing what a million of something looked like—there were 937,000 caps in the bin. According to eyewitnesses, the fire was first noticed near the center of the building and spread throughout the structure within seconds. All students, teachers, and staff were safely evacuated. The students "wouldn't have done nearly so well in a fire drill," said one teacher. "If it had been practice, they'd have been playing and pushing each other, but no one panicked, and no one got hurt."

Girl Scout Troop 562, shown here, met from 1956 to 1963. Leaders were Bernice Roberts and Hazel Bradley. "Having served as a WAVE in the US Navy, mother brought her love of the military to our troop," said Paula Bradley Jones. "Songs, camping, crafts and the Girl Scout Pledge . . . these are happy memories that last a lifetime!" Shown here are, from left to right, (first row) Sally Norris, Diana Roberts, Becky Harrell, Lynne Handley, and Rhonda Pannell; (second row) Sterling Pierce, Judy Russell, Karen LaRoque, Lynda Hendrix, Mary White, Dorcus Mashburn, and Gayle Robinson; (third row) Bernice Roberts, Peggy Homan, Laura Greene, Paula Bradley, Joy Smith, Linda Bradley, Pam Hall, Sue Richie, and Hazel Bradley. The girls wearing sashes had begun earning badges, a collection of which ultimately became a record of a member's adventures and accomplishments as a Girl Scout.

Longtime Trussville resident Hazel Bradley, a native of Water Valley, Mississippi, served as a WAVE during World War II. She enlisted in the Navy on June 27, 1944, and headed off to boot camp at the Hunter College Naval Training Station in New York City. Afterward, she attended Yeoman School at Oklahoma A&M (now Oklahoma State) before being assigned to active duty at Treasure Island, San Francisco, where she spent the rest of her military career performing clerical duties. She was honorably discharged as a yeoman first class on April 3, 1946. Back in the South, she landed a job at the Social Security Administration (SSA) office in New Orleans, where she met native Texan and fellow SSA employee Winston Bradley. They soon married, and the young couple wound up being transferred to the SSA's Birmingham office. Upon the recommendation of commuting coworkers, they bought a home in Trussville's Cahaba Project area, where they ultimately raised four children: sons Winston and Chuck and twin daughters Paula and Linda. (Courtesy of the Bradley family.)

Today's Trussville Sports Complex (TSC) is a far cry from the more limited athletic facilities of earlier eras. While places like the Whaley "Pop" Hall ball fields and the Cahaba Project tennis courts long served the city well, as Trussville has grown so has the demand for larger and more up-to-date places to play. A multi-sports complex, TSC is home to the Trussville Racquet Club, soccer fields, baseball fields (top), softball fields (bottom), and a youth football field. The complex is also home to a wooded network of bicycle and hiking trails, some of which run along the Cahaba River. The trails run for nearly five miles around the perimeter of the park and offer a peaceful, off-road fitness alternative for those who enjoy walking, running, and biking. (Courtesy of Trussville Utilities.)

Before the Trussville Sports Complex opened in the early 1990s, boys played baseball at the old fields off Cherokee Drive (current location of the Trussville Senior Activities Center), and girls played just across the Cahaba River at the softball fields behind Masonic Park. Names like Braves, Dodgers, Red Sox, White Sox, and Pirates identified the teams with their professional counterparts, and each local player had personal favorites in the big leagues. On this page, the 1960 Colts (above) and the 1964 Cardinals (below) pose for the requisite team portraits. (Below, courtesy of Laurie McLendon Nabors.)

The Trussville Swimming Pool was completed and opened for business in June 1954. The cost of the pool, excluding land, was $50,000. The pool holds 127,000 gallons of water, and until a warming re-circulatory system was installed in 1996, it was filled with bone-chilling springwater. The 1954 pool house was replaced in 2007, and a splash park was added in 2008.

Over the years, many a swim team, much like the championship 1957 Trussville Aquatic Club, has competed at the Trussville Swimming Pool. When this photograph was snapped, the team had a three-year unbeaten record in state swimming and diving competitions. In 2010, team member Jim Robinson (back row, third from the left) swept the swimming categories for males age 70 and over at the 2013 Alabama Sports Festival. (Courtesy of Jim Robinson.)

This photograph shows the Trussville Swimming Pool in relation to the original Hewitt-Trussville High School. The surrounding area, with its grassy malls, tennis courts, co-op building (now Heritage Hall), and other public facilities, was the focal point of the Cahaba Project community when it was first built. In many ways, it remains so today. So, when it came to building a community swimming pool, choosing the location was easy. Even after 60 years, it is proving to be the right choice. Residents still gather on the nearby mall area for festivals, celebrations, and other activities, and it is during those times and in that place that Trussville's sense of community is strongest. With a future restoration of the old school for elementary use and plans under way to expand the present Trussville Library facilities, located just down the street, the "anchor" area of the Cahaba Project is bound to continue as the heart of Trussville for many years to come. (Courtesy of Trussville Historical Archives.)

While no one remembers exactly what Paul Bradford Jr. (left) and Paul Bradford Sr. are doing in their backyard garden—perhaps picking vegetables or pulling weeds—many longtime Trussville residents would recognize their backdrop as the old Hewitt Elementary School. The Bradford family lived next door to the school, just a block or two off Main Street. (Courtesy of Gloria Bradford Forehand.)

When organized sports were not available, and the pool was closed, Trussville children of an earlier era had to get creative. These kids are not only doing a great job of occupying themselves without the benefit of video games or iPhones, they are also proving that, with a paper crown and a regal-looking bedspread robe, even a small-town girl can be queen for a day. (Courtesy of Imelda Gilmer.)

Some people show their school spirit by cheering and waving pom-poms, and others show it, well, in less conventional ways. No one knows exactly to whom these painted posteriors belong, except maybe the owners themselves. And, over 65 years later, even they may have forgotten which backside belongs to which girl. At any rate, none of them are likely to come rushing forward to proclaim their identity at this late date. If they do, we hope to hear about it. Whoever they are, and however this photograph came to be, the *Memento* yearbook staff obviously considered it a fitting signoff for the 1947 edition; it appears on the last page. We shall follow suit and likewise feature as our finale these young ladies posing bottom-side-up on the front porch of Hewitt-Trussville High School. We hope readers get as big a kick as we have over this photograph, which we have affectionately named *The Ends*. (Courtesy of Trussville Public Library.)

Visit us at
arcadiapublishing.com